Simple Maths

Sharing and Dividing

Richard Leffingwell

Raintree

www.raintreepublishers.co.uk
Visit our website to find out more information about **Raintree** books.

To order:
☎ Phone 44 (0) 1865 888112
▤ Send a fax to 44 (0) 1865 314091
▢ Visit the Raintree Bookshop at **www.raintreepublishers.co.uk** to browse our catalogue and order online.

First published in Great Britain by Raintree, Halley Court, Jordan Hill, Oxford OX2 8EJ, part of Harcourt Education.
Raintree is a registered trademark of Harcourt Education Ltd.

Editorial: Diyan Leake and Cassie Mayer
Design: Joanna Hinton-Malivoire and
  The Partnership
Picture Research: Erica Newbery
Production: Duncan Gilbert

Originated by Modern Age
Printed and bound in China by
  South China Printing Company

10 digit ISBN 1 4062 0393 9 (hardback)
13 digit ISBN 978 1 4062 0393 6
10 09 08 07 06
10 9 8 7 6 5 4 3 2 1

10 digit ISBN 1 4062 0398 X (paperback)
13 digit ISBN 978 1 4062 0398 1
11 10 09 08 07
10 9 8 7 6 5 4 3 2 1

British Library Cataloguing in Publication Data
Leffingwell, Richard
Sharing and Dividing
513.2'14
A full catalogue record for this book is available from the British Library.

Acknowledgements
The publishers would like to thank the following for permission to reproduce photographs: Getty Images (Photodisc Red/Davies & Starr) pp. **4, 5, 6, 7, 8**; Harcourt Education Ltd (www.mmstudios.co.uk) pp. **9–20, 22**, back cover; Photolibrary (Brand X/Burke Triolo) p. **21**

Cover photograph reproduced with permission of Harcourt Education Ltd (www.mmstudios.co.uk).

The publishers would like to thank Patti Barber, Specialist in Early Childhood and Primary Education, Institute of Education, University of London, for her assistance in the preparation of this book.

Every effort has been made to contact copyright holders of any material reproduced in this book. Any omissions will be rectified in subsequent printings if notice is given to the publishers.

The paper used to print this book comes from sustainable resources.

Contents

What is sharing?

You and a friend find 6 shells on the beach.

You want to share the shells.

How many shells does each
person get?

Pass the shells out one at a time.

Do this until all of the shells
are gone.

Each person gets 3 shells.

They each get a fair share.

$$6 \div 2 = 3$$

Sharing something out is a way of dividing.

To make a fair share, you have to divide things equally.

Sharing flowers

What if you had 9 flowers and 3 vases?

How could you divide them equally?

First you put 1 flower in each vase.

You still have 6 flowers left.

Then you put another flower in each vase.

You still have 3 flowers left.

Put another flower in each vase.

Now all of the vases have the same number of flowers.

$$9 \div 3 = 3$$

You divided 9 flowers into 3 vases.

Each vase has 3 flowers.

Sharing cars

You and a friend have 6 toy cars.

How many will you have if you share them equally?

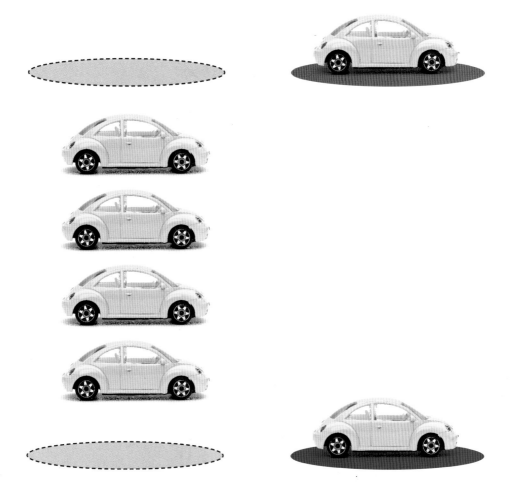

You start by each taking 1 toy car.

There are still 4 toy cars left.

You keep taking one car each until they are divided equally.

You each get three toy cars.

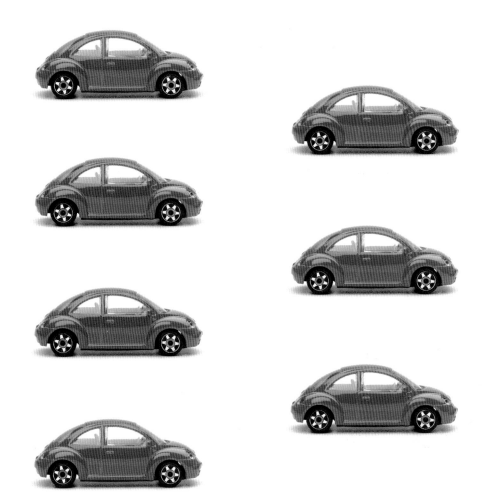

What would you do if you had 7 toy cars to share with your friend?

Each of you would get 3 toy cars.

There would be 1 left over.

What should you do with the extra toy car?

You could give it to another friend.

You could save it until you have another one to share equally.

Practising dividing

Dividing is useful when you need to share a group of things.

When have you divided things?

Quiz

You have 8 pencils.

How many will there be in each of the 2 pots?

Make sure each pot gets a fair share!

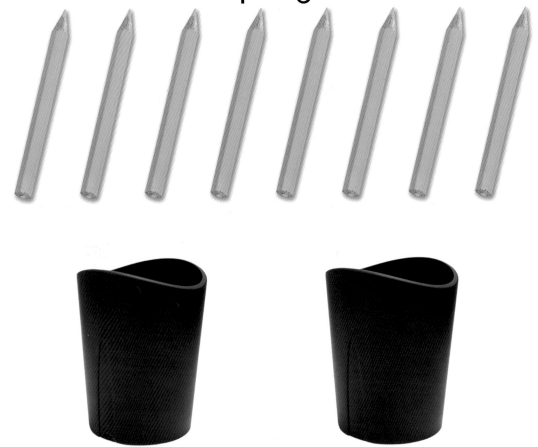

The "divided by" sign

÷

You use this sign to show that you are dividing one number by another.

$$4 \div 2$$

When you divide 4 by 2, you get 2.

=

You use the equals sign to show what 4 divided by 2 is equal to.

$$4 \div 2 = 2$$

Index

Answer to the quiz on page 22
There will be 4 pencils in each pot.

Note to parents and teachers
Reading non-fiction texts for information is an important part of a child's literacy development. Readers can be encouraged to ask simple questions and then use the text to find the answers. Most chapters in this book begin with a question. Read the questions together. Look at the pictures. Talk about what the answer might be. Then read the text to find out if your predictions were correct. To develop readers' enquiry skills, encourage them to think of other questions they might ask about the topic. Discuss where you could find the answers. Assist children in using the contents page, picture glossary and index to practise research skills and new vocabulary.